Conte

G000039691

This book belongs to

Say the Sounds

y
as in
silly

i_e
as in
kite

e_e
as in
these

o_e
as in
rose

a_e
as in
cake

u_e
as in
cube

**Spot the
Story Setting**

sunken ship

wood

bedroom

underground

cliffs

mountain

The Three Billy Goats Gruff

The three Billy Goats Gruff lived on a farm at the bottom of a mountain.

Every morning, the three Billy Goats
Gruff ran up the side of the mountain
to go and graze, but they had to stop
when they got to the river.

In the river, there was an ugly old troll who lived under some wooden planks. The troll was angry all the time and he never let the three Billy Goats Gruff cross the river.

The troll yelled and shouted if the
three Billy Goats Gruff went too close
to his wooden planks. Whenever an
animal tried to cross the planks, the
troll jumped up and flashed his long,
sharp teeth.

The three Billy Goats Gruff looked longingly at the bank on the far side of the river.

"If only we can get across the river, we can go to the top of the mountain. There is a lot more food on that side of the river," said the biggest Billy Goat Gruff.

"Come along, then," said the smallest Billy Goat Gruff. "I bet I can run across so quickly that the troll will not see me."

The biggest Billy Goat Gruff tried to stop him, but the smallest Billy Goat Gruff started running. Trip, trap, trip, trap went his hooves on the wooden planks.

The ugly old troll started to roar and shout when the smallest Billy Goat Gruff set off across the planks.

"GET OFF MY PLANKS!" he roared. "You cannot cross the river. I will chomp you and munch you up for dinner," and he snapped his long, sharp teeth at the smallest Billy Goat Gruff.

The smallest Billy Goat Gruff was so afraid that he started to shake. "Do not munch me up for dinner!" he cried. "I am too small to make a good dinner for a big troll like you. A much bigger billy goat will come by in a little while."

"Hmm, you are quite small," muttered the troll, rubbing his chin and looking at the next goat. As he did so, the smallest Billy Goat Gruff slipped quickly across the planks.

The second Billy Goat Gruff said,
"If the smallest Billy Goat Gruff can
get across the river, then so can I!"
He started to run across the wooden
planks - trip, trap, trip, trap
went his hooves.

Up jumped the troll again, shouting.
"Mmmm! DINNER!" he cried, and
rubbed his belly. "I like goat for
dinner," he smiled.

The second Billy Goat Gruff waited
for the troll to finish shouting.
Then he said, "Do not have me for
dinner. I am too small to make much
of a dinner for a big troll like you. The
biggest Billy Goat Gruff will come by
soon, and he will make a much better
dinner for a troll of your size."

"Mmmm," said the troll, rubbing his
chin and licking his lips as he looked
across at the biggest Billy Goat Gruff.
As he did so, the second Billy Goat
Gruff ran quickly across the planks.

As the biggest Billy Goat Gruff came along, the troll yelled and stamped and shook his fists.

"I shall munch you and chomp you and have you for my dinner!" he shouted, and smiled so that the sun shone on all his big, sharp teeth.

"NO, YOU WILL NOT!" shouted the biggest Billy Goat Gruff, and he snorted and stamped his hooves. He shook his horns at the troll and then started to run. TRIP, TRAP, TRIP, TRAP went his heavy hooves on the wooden planks.

The troll shouted and stamped and gnashed his teeth. The biggest Billy Goat Gruff snorted and ran at the troll. His big hard horns butted into the troll, who went spinning up and up and up, and then...

SPLASH! The troll landed in the river.
He bobbed up again and spluttered as
he tried to shout, but the river swept
him off. He waved his arms and shook
his fists as he was dragged around a
bend in the river.

The biggest Billy Goat Gruff ran safely across the planks. All three Billy Goats Gruff were so glad that the troll had gone that they jumped about. "You were so brave!" cried the smallest Billy Goat Gruff, hugging the biggest one, and the three goats ran happily on, up to the top of the mountain.

As for the troll, he was never seen on
that mountain again. He found a dark
cave in some rocks where he made
his home, and he never stamped and
shouted or tried to have goat
for dinner again.

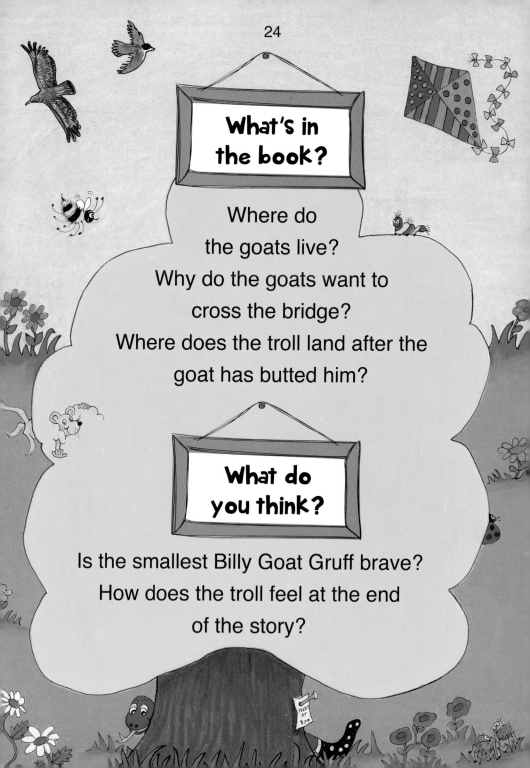

What's in the book?

Where do
the goats live?
Why do the goats want to
cross the bridge?
Where does the troll land after the
goat has butted him?

What do you think?

Is the smallest Billy Goat Gruff brave?
How does the troll feel at the end
of the story?

The Fox and the Stork

In a wood next to a big river, there
lived a fox and a stork. One morning,
they met on the bank of the river.
"Come and have some dinner with me,"
said the fox to the stork.
"Yes, thank you, I will," replied the stork.

So the fox set about cooking dinner.
He mixed, cut, chopped and added
until he had made a big pot of food.
"Mmmm, that smells good," said the
fox. He looked into the pot
and licked his lips.

When the stork arrived, she said,
"Mmmm, that smells good. I did not
catch much fish this morning,
so I am very hungry."

The fox and the stork sat down to
dinner. The fox spooned out the food
onto the big, flat plates he had set out.

The stork pecked at the food with her long, pointed bill, but it was hard for her as the plate was so flat. She pecked and pecked, but she only ate a little of her food.

When he had finished his dinner,
the fox licked his lips.
"Mmmm, that was good," he said.
"Have you finished?" he added,
looking at the stork's plate.

"My bill is too long and pointed for this
big, flat plate," the stork explained.
She was still very hungry, and it made
her angry when the fox quickly ate all
the food she had left as well.

The next week, when the fox came to the river bank, he found the stork there, waiting for him.

"Will you come and have dinner with me this evening?" she said.
"Yes, thank you, I will," said the fox, licking his lips greedily.
"I am so glad," said the stork politely, but she smiled to herself.

This time, it was the stork who cooked
the dinner. She mixed, cut, chopped
and added until she had
made a big pot of food.
"Mmmm," the stork said to herself.
"That smells good."

When the fox arrived,
he sniffed the food cooking.
"Mmmm," he said, "that smells good.
I am hungry," and he rubbed his belly.

The stork and the fox sat down to dinner. The stork spooned out the food into the tall, thin jars she had set out.

The fox tried to lick his food out of
the top of the jar, but it was hard for
him as the jar was so tall and thin.
He licked and licked, but he only ate
a little of his food.

He had to sit and see the stork peck up
all her dinner with her long, thin bill.
"Mmmm. That was good," she said.
"Have you finished?" she added,
looking at all the food the fox had left.

"I cannot lick more. This jar is too tall
and thin for me," he explained.

The greedy fox was angry when the
stork finished up the rest of the food
in his jar. He still felt hungry as
he had had so little dinner.

"Well," the stork said, "I was upset when I came to dinner with you, and you gave me a big, flat plate."

"I am sorry," the fox said. "It was wrong of me. Come and have dinner with me again next week, and this time will be different."

So next week, the stork went to have dinner with the fox again. Before she arrived, the fox chopped, cut, added and mixed, until he had a big pot of food.

"Mmmm, that smells good," he said.

When the stork arrived, she smiled
and said, "That smells good."
"Thank you. Come and sit down,"
said the fox.

He set out a big, flat plate for himself
again, but he gave the stork a tall, thin
jar. This time she had no problem
getting at her food, and she ate plenty!

What's in the book?

Why does the
stork find it hard
to eat off the plate?
Why does the fox find it hard to
eat from the jar?
What happens the next time they
have dinner together?

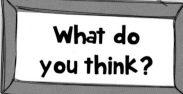

What do you think?

Why does the stork give the fox a jar
to eat from?
Which dinner do they both enjoy the most?

The Outing

Just before home time, Miss Beech gives
all the children a letter.
"This letter is about our outing,"
she explains.
The children rush out with the letters.
"We are going on an outing!" they shout.

On the morning of the outing, the children arrive at school in boots and raincoats. They are all carrying lunchboxes. Miss Beech and the helpers hurry all the children onto the bus. Miss Beech has a bucket and a box of equipment.

Anna, Bill and Seth sit at the back of the bus. They wave to the cars as they drive along.

When they arrive, Miss Beech, the helpers and the children get off the bus and someone comes to greet them. She tells them her name is Roz.

Then she tells them to come down to the study barn, where they dump all the bags, lunchboxes and raincoats. Next, Roz tells them what they are going to do.

The children split up, and Bill, Seth and Anna go with Roz to the pond. They are going to do pond dipping. They have some nets and some flat plastic boxes.

They stand on a wooden platform and dip the nets into the pond. They sweep the nets about in the pond and then they empty the contents into the boxes.

They catch caddis flies and lots of tadpoles. Some of the bigger tadpoles have got legs. They catch a lot of pond weed too!

Suddenly, Anna's net slips out of her wet hands. It floats on top of the pond.

"Help!" shouts Anna. "I have lost my net." Roz takes Bill's net and hooks up Anna's one with it. The children all clap as she gives it back.
"Thank you," Anna smiles.

Meg, Gus and Hinda go pond dipping
with Roz. Anna, Bill and Seth
go with a man called Mark,
who takes them on a forest trail.

They go around the trail looking for
markers with different animals on.
Then the children do a quiz about the
animals and where they live.

Next all the children meet up again
for lunch. They go down to the
bottom of some cliffs, where they sit
down on the sand and have a picnic.

When everyone has finished, Roz sends the children off to look for interesting things.

"Keep a look out for lucky stones, like this one," she tells them, and out of her pocket she takes a stone with a hole in it.

When the children get back, Roz is waiting for them. She has sticky-backed plastic and three boxes with different sorts of sand inside.

The children make sand hand-prints by cutting out hand shapes from the sticky-backed plastic and scattering the different sands onto them to make patterns.

The children stick the hand-prints onto card and cut them out. Roz gives out sticks and bits of string, and tells everyone to use the string to tie the hand-prints onto the sticks.

Next they tie all the interesting things
they found onto the sticks as well, to
make wall hangings. Roz explains that
when the hangings are finished, the
children can take them home.

The children look at what they have found and start to make the hangings. They cut, tie and knot. When they have finished, they look at the hangings with Roz and Miss Beech.

Meg's stick has a big feather, a green stone and some shells. Bill's has a twisted bit of driftwood and a float from a fishing net.

"These are very good," Roz tells them.

Hinda's stick has lots of shells and a bit of rope. Anna is very proud of her hanging. She has found some driftwood that she thinks looks like a boat, and under her sand hand-print she has tied a lucky stone!

What's in the book?

Who greets the
children when they get off the bus?
What do they catch in the pond?
Where do they have their lunch?

What do you think?

Are the children excited about the outing?
How does the stone get a hole in it?

The Little Merman

The mermen were having a game of
finball. They had strong tails which
they used to flip the ball as they tried
to score goals into clam shells. At the
sides of the pitch stood some supporters,
who were cheering the mermen on.

One little merman, called Sol, was too young to join in so he made up a different game. He had to toss a shell into the waves and his pet dogfish, Chips, had to swim off and bring it back to him.

Sol tossed a shell and it floated into
a thick forest of weeds. Chips dashed
into the weeds to fetch it. Sol waited,
but when Chips did not come back, he
swam up to the forest of weeds and
called his name.

When Chips still did not come back,
Sol swam into the weed forest to look
for him. It was green and gloomy
there, and the little merman felt afraid.

"Chips!" he called again.

Chips still did not come back but Sol
had an odd feeling that something
or someone was looking at him. He
looked around but there was no one
to be seen. He shook his head and
swam bravely on.

SNAP went some big, sharp teeth, but
Sol did not see them.

Then he spotted a shell, like the one
he had been tossing for Chips, and
ducked down to pick it up.
SNAP went the big, sharp teeth again,
just where Sol had been swimming,
but still he did not see them.

Then Sol spotted a tail sticking out from some weeds. He sped off to see if the tail belonged to Chips.

SNAP went the big, sharp teeth again, just where Sol had been standing, but still he did not see them.

"Chips!" called Sol, as he swam up to where the tail had been. "Chips!" He was just in time to see the tail swimming off. Sol took a deep breath and swam on into the weeds.

SNAP went the big, sharp teeth again, just where Sol had been, but still he did not see them.

Sol was just in time to see the tail shoot
into a small hole in the side of a sunken
ship. He swam up to it and peeped into
the hole. It was dark inside the ship.

"Chips," called Sol softly.

Suddenly, he spotted a long, dark shape waiting in the weeds. The long, dark shape was looking at him and the long, dark shape had big, sharp, snapping teeth!

Sol was terrified and shot into the hole in the side of the sunken ship.

SNAP went the big, sharp teeth again, just outside the hole where Sol had been, but just too late to catch him.

Safe inside the ship, Sol swam to the far corner of the cabin, sat down, and looked around. There was an old cannon, some timbers from the deck and a chest in one corner.

Then Sol spotted a little head peeping out of the chest.

"Chips!" he called, and Chips slithered out and swam across to Sol. The little dogfish was so happy to see him that he swam around and around his friend until they were quite dizzy.

Sol gave his pet a big hug. Just then, the cabin shook and a pointed nose slammed into the hole in the side of the ship. It was a long nose with big, sharp teeth. It was a shark!

Chips started to shake.
"Help!" Sol called.

The little merman looked around. He tried not to panic, but there was not much time, as the wooden ship was old and the shark was strong.
"Help me!" Sol called to Chips.

Chips helped him to drag the cannon to the hole. The shark tried to ram into the side of the ship again, but this time his pointed snout got stuck inside the cannon.
"Quick!" shouted Sol to Chips. "Swim!"

Sol and Chips swam very quickly.
They did not stop until they got safely
back to the finball pitch, where the
game was just ending. Sol's dad was
one of the winners! Sol swam up to
him and gave his dad a big hug.

"I am sorry the game took so long,"
said his dad. "Were you very bored?"
Sol gave Chips a quick wink.
"Not very," he replied.

What's in the book?

What game do the mermen play?
Where does Chips hide?
What does the shark get stuck in?

What do you think?

What creature watches Sol
amongst the weeds?
Is Sol's dad worried about him
during the game?

The Cricket and the Ants

It was summer and the sun
shone down on a cricket,
who leapt and skipped about.
"What fun!" he cried, as he landed
beside a bee. "What are you doing?"
"Collecting pollen," replied the bee, "to
make food to store in our hive."

"Food to store?" said the cricket.
"Whatever for? What a silly Bee," he
added in a whisper as he leapt off.

From morning until evening, he
continued to have fun, jumping and
hopping about and singing happy,
summery tunes with his long, back legs.

Next morning, the cricket sat looking on as some ants rushed back and forth, collecting seeds and carrying them back to the anthill.

"What are you doing?" said the cricket. "Collecting food and storing it for the winter," the ants replied.

The cricket scoffed at them.
"You silly ants!" he cried. "Look around you. There is plenty of food. Winter will not come for a long time, so why not just have fun like me? Let me entertain you with a tune," he offered, and he used his long, back legs like a fiddle to make a merry tune for them.

"No, thank you," said the ants. "We must collect as much food as we can, or else we will starve in the long winter."

"What silly ants," muttered the cricket, and he shook his head as they marched off. He just did not understand why everyone was so boring.

All summer long, the cricket continued to have fun. There was still plenty of food about and he did not see the point of bothering about winter yet.

"Morning, bees," he'd call and wave. "Morning, ants. Haven't you finished all that storing yet?" and he'd shake his head at them.

Then, one morning, the weather
started to get chilly.

"Winter will be here soon!" cried the
cricket. "I suppose I had better start
collecting some food."
But when he looked around, there
was not much food left.

He collected a small store of seeds
and hid them in a hole in a tree.
"That will do," he muttered. "I do not
need much food in winter and I can
look for some more if I run out."

As the winter went on, the weather got colder and colder, and the cricket felt more and more unhappy.

"I am too cold to sing," he said sadly, as he sat shivering. "It is so cold that I am all out of tune."

Then, one morning, he woke up feeling
very hungry. He helped himself to a seed
and sat and ate it, shivering. It did not
fill him up, so soon he stretched out his
arm for more, but his hole was empty.
He had used up all of his store of seeds!

All this time, the ants had been snug
and happy under the ground.
They still had plenty of food left, and
they were planning a party. They had
sorted out some party games, but there
was still something missing.

"We need something to listen to!"
they said.

Just then, one of the ants remembered
the cricket who had offered to amuse
them in the summer.

"Perhaps he will come and entertain
us," they said, and some of them
set out to look for him.
"Brrr!" they said and shivered.
"It is freezing out here."

When the cricket spotted the ants,
he hid from them.
"They will see that all my food has
gone," he said to himself. "Then they
will blame me for having fun all summer
instead of collecting food like they did.

"Cricket! Cricket!" called the ants, but
the cricket kept hidden, sadly waiting
for them to go. Then, just when they
were about to give up, one of the ants
spotted him.

The cricket was thrilled to go with the ants into the snug nest and to join the party. The ants gave him a big plate of food and he was so happy that he fiddled tunes for hours. But when the party was finished, he looked sadly out of the anthill at the wind and rain outside.

"Thank you so much for having me," he said humbly, as he got ready to go. "It was a good party."

The ants looked at the cricket and then
around at the snug nest.
"Cricket, why not spend the rest of the
winter down here with us?" they said.
"We will give you food if you
will entertain us."

The cricket smiled and nodded happily.

So, for the rest of that winter, the
cricket lived underground with the ants.
He was no longer lonely, freezing and
hungry. Instead, he had lots of friends,
a snug bed and plenty of food until
summer came around again.

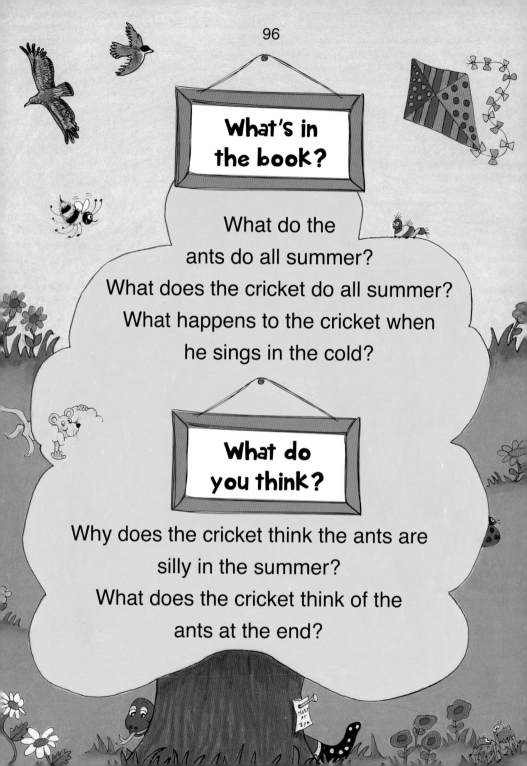

What's in the book?

What do the
ants do all summer?
What does the cricket do all summer?
What happens to the cricket when
he sings in the cold?

What do you think?

Why does the cricket think the ants are
silly in the summer?
What does the cricket think of the
ants at the end?

Little Monsters

Monster verse

Monsters in a cap.
Monsters in a cape.
Monster in a hat
that the monsters hate.

This monster has a pet.
His name is Pete.
He likes to be fed
a sack of feed.

Monsters have a bit
and monsters have a bite.
Monsters make a din
when the monsters dine.

This monster had a rod
and down he rode.
To get a cod,
according to the code.

Look at us
and what we can use.
Monster cubs
spell with monster cubes.

Instead of "said"

No monster ever said a thing.
Instead of "said" they wailed and yelled.
"Mine," wailed sister monster loudly.
"Keep out," yelled her monster twin.

Big Monster came
to referee.
"Stop!" she hollered
at the twins.
"What is going on?" she cried,
and waited 'til the shouting died.

Big Monster looked at little monsters.
Little monsters tried again.
"It was not me," they wailed.
"It was her/him," they whined.

Big Monster held her hand up.
"Hush, shshshsh!" she called.
"What a noise and hubbub,
what a racket and a fuss."

"Wail, mutter, sob and moan.
He has my teddy," she complained.
"Hiss, grunt, snarl and groan.
She has my car," he yelped.

"Give them back," snapped Big Monster,
"by the time that I count ten."
"1, 2, 3, 4, 5," she whispered,
"6, 7, 8, 9, **10**," she yelled.

Little sister monster twin
gave back the model car.
"Thank you," barked her monster twin
and cried, "so here you are."

Big Monster looked at them and nodded.
"That's better, then," she smiled.
"No more yapping, cackling, snarling.
Do not utter a single sound."

She held up a long pointed finger
and wagged her talon at the twins.
"No more noise and scrapping
or I will send you to your room!"

All was tranquil for some seconds.
Big Monster had just sat down,
when "MINE" cried one little monster twin.
"No mine!" the sister replied.

"That's it," snarled Big Monster.
"That's all that I can take.
I will go up to your room."
CRASH! The door slammed shut.

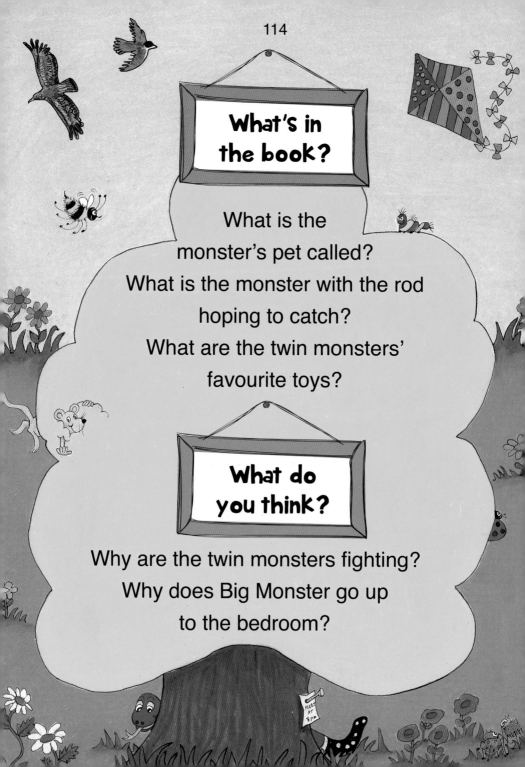

What's in the book?

What is the
monster's pet called?
What is the monster with the rod
hoping to catch?
What are the twin monsters'
favourite toys?

What do you think?

Why are the twin monsters fighting?
Why does Big Monster go up
to the bedroom?

Parents

An important part of becoming a confident, fluent reader is a child's ability to understand what they are reading. Below are some suggestions on how to develop a child's reading comprehension.

Make reading this book a shared experience between you and the child. Try to avoid leaving it until the whole book is read before talking about it. Occasionally stop at various intervals throughout the book.

Ask questions about the characters, the setting, the action and the meaning.

Encourage the child to think about what might happen next. It does not matter if the answer is right or wrong, so long as the suggestion makes sense and demonstrates understanding.

Ask the child to describe what is happening in the illustrations.

Relate what is happening in the book to any real-life experiences the child may have.

Pick out any vocabulary that may be new to the child and ask what they think it means. If they don't know, explain it and relate it to what is happening in the book.

Encourage the child to summarise, in their own words, what they have read.

Book Review

Try to answer these questions about each story in this book:

What was the story about?

What happened at the end of the story? Did you guess what was going to happen?

What was your favourite part of the story? Why did you like it?

Which character did you like the best? Can you describe them?

Did you like the illustrations? Why?

Did any parts of the story make you laugh?

Do you think anyone you know would enjoy this book?

Could you re-tell the story in your own words?

Has anything similar to this story ever happened to you?

Would you have liked this story to be shorter or longer?

Were there any parts of the story that you didn't like?

Have you read any stories that are similar to this one?

Would you enjoy reading this story again and would you recommend it to a friend?

Character Review

Choose a character in this book to think about:

What is their name?

Do you know where they live?

Describe what they look like.

What do they do in the story?

Are they good or bad? Why?

Do you like them? Why?

What other things would you like to know about them?